SCOTTISH MASTER

The National Galleries of Scotland, in its three buildings, the Portrait Gallery, the National Gallery and the Gallery of Modern Art, holds the nation's collection of Scottish art. It is a marvellously rich and varied collection ranging in date from the 16th century to the present day, including works by artists of world stature and by others hardly known outside the Galleries themselves.

SCOTTISH MASTERS is a new series designed to make some of the most interesting and delightful Scottish artists more widely known. In 1984 the Patrons of the National Galleries of Scotland was founded under the Presidency of HRH The Duke of Edinburgh to channel extra financial assistance from the private sector to the National Galleries. They are enormously grateful to the Scottish Post Office Board for the generous sponsorship of this series. This has enabled these attractively designed monographs to be published at such a reasonable price. How appropriate that the masters of communications themselves should help us to communicate to Scotland, and beyond, the heritage of us all.

Explanation is an essential part of the Galleries' purpose: so also is acquisition. We are doubly grateful to the Scottish Post Office Board for the generous financial help they have given us to boost our active policy of purchasing the finest works of Scottish art for our national collections. We are delighted that the Board share our view that for a lively gallery acquisition and explanation must go hand in hand.

The Scottish Post Office Board's imaginative support of the National Galleries is just one part of their enlightened programme of involvement with both the visual and performing arts, reminding us of the central role that the Post Office plays in Scottish life.

THE VISCOUNT WEIR,
Chairman of the Patrons of the National Galleries of Scotland.

ANGUS GROSSART,
Chairman of the Trustees of the National Galleries of Scotland.

Self Portrait, 1916
Oil on canvas, 50.8 x 40.6 cm
(Scottish National Portrait Gallery)

William McCANCE

1894-1970

BY PATRICK ELLIOTT

WILLIAM McCANCE

Painter, sculptor, printmaker, typographer, book designer, art critic, essayist, teacher: these are some of the epithets that one might use to describe William McCance. A man of great intellectual ability and prodigious artistic talent, he had a marvellous disregard for conventional career structures and rather than focus his efforts on one activity alone, chose instead to follow a variety of pursuits. Had he concentrated on painting or printmaking he would no doubt have achieved greater renown. Nevertheless, what remains is an extraordinary life, full of incident and notable achievements. His highly stylized compositions of the 1920s count among the most remarkable British paintings of the period while the books produced at the Gregynog Press in Wales, under his control in the early 1930s, are perhaps the finest quality publications to appear in Britain between the wars. It is surprising that an artist of his stature has, despite a sprinkling of exhibitions in recent years, passed into the realms of obscurity.

Fig 1
NEAR TARBERT, LOCH FYNE
1914. Oil on wood, 23 x 30 cm
(Private Collection)

McCance's mother, Elizabeth MacBride, was from an Ayrshire weaving family while his father, James McCance, was an Ulsterman who had come to Scotland in search of work. The couple settled in Cambuslang in the south of Glasgow where William was born in 1894, the seventh of eight children. His father, who worked in the local colliery, was killed in a mining accident in 1911, the year in which William McCance entered Glasgow School of Art. His early interest in drawing had been encouraged by an elder brother who was an engraver, but otherwise there was no particular family interest or involvement in the arts. An early painting of 1914, *Near Tarbert, Loch Fyne* (fig 1), executed at the age of twenty, shows evident skill but hardly indicates the dramatic turn his art would take just a few years later. McCance graduated in 1915 and then took a teacher training course at Glasgow's Kennedy Street School, gaining his qualifications at the end of 1916.

Instead of going into teaching as he might have wished, the next few years were passed in a more unexpected manner. A conscientious objector, McCance was imprisoned in November 1917 for refusing to go on parade with the Scottish Rifles at Hamilton Barracks. Following spells at Wormwood Scrubs, Knutsford Prison and Dartmoor he was transferred to Warwick prison, where, due to his art school education, he was put in charge of re-painting the buildings. He later recalled that one of his tasks was to oversee the conversion of the inebriates section into a home for 'immoral girls'. A more onerous duty was to demolish the prison gallows, a business which affected him deeply.

In July 1918 McCance was given leave to marry Agnes Miller Parker (fig 2) whom he had met at Glasgow School of Art, and who in the 1930s developed into one of Britain's leading wood engravers. When McCance was discharged from the army in March 1920, the couple moved to London, taking a flat in Earl's Court.[1] Miller Parker taught at a school in Gerrard's Cross from 1920 to 1928 and then at Clapham High School while McCance lectured at schools and evening institutes in London and produced cartoons and art criticism for various magazines. The years were evidently difficult ones economically, for although both were producing oil paintings and prints at the time, they seem to have sold little if anything at all.

Fig 2
PORTRAIT OF AGNES MILLER PARKER
1918. Pencil on paper, 34 x 24 cm
(Private Collection)

McCance's paintings of the twenties occupy a unique place in Scottish art. With the exception of William Johnstone, no other Scottish painter responded with such imagination and vigour to the Cubist and Surrealist movements which had emerged in France in the preceding years. It is not clear precisely when McCance first began working in a semi-abstract style or quite how these works developed from the more conventional studies he had produced in Glasgow. A few paintings done in a neo-impressionist vein exist (plate 1), perhaps marking a transition from the early, naturalistic idiom to a more stylized one – though this is far from certain. It has been suggested that McCance made his first semi-abstract paintings in 1920 but this has not been proven, and the earliest dated works of this kind are of 1922.[2] However, those paintings which are dated 1922 are highly resolved and demanding works which may well have been preceded by preliminary experiments, begun perhaps a year or two earlier. In the absence of further evidence, one can only say that McCance had arrived at a highly stylized form of painting by about 1922.

The small oil, *Primeval Movement* (plate 2), is inscribed by the artist on the back 'Earliest Abstract experiment Painting, using pure colour as form-expressing medium', but is undated. The brightly-coloured forms suggest plant-like tendrils and also recall motifs found in *art nouveau* designs. The painting appears at first to be entirely abstract, but the image is in fact based on a stylized clay-slip sculpture of a cat that McCance himself had made (fig 3). The cat form appears twice in the painting: in the centre and in the larger form enveloping it, with the head in the top

Fig 3
CAT
c. 1921–2. Clayslip (glazed), 7 x 9.3 x 6.5 cm
(Private Collection)

right corner. It may well represent a mother cat protecting its kitten – a theme McCance (who was inordinately fond of cats) treated in a more easily decipherable style in later years.

The faceted cat motif reappears, again twice, in a much larger and more resolved painting, *Conflict* (plate 3) of 1922, where it is seen in the foreground area, viewed from both the side and from behind. The rest of the painting is difficult to read but represents a stylized landscape with mountains in the distance and a tree trunk at the right, its branches dominating the top part of the picture. The tall vertical form in the centre is a straightforward depiction of a sculpture (now lost) made by the artist, and this seems to be repeated on the left of the picture, though from a different angle. An inventory of the picture's contents is wholly at odds with the experience of looking at the actual painting, for McCance has conjured up an extraordinary sense of organic growth and electric tension from such mundane sources. The effect of this vividly coloured work (sadly, much of its impact is lost in black and white reproduction) is of sinister, primeval life-forms inhabiting a bizarre and alien landscape.

The forms in the 1922 *Heavy Structures in a Landscape Setting* (plate 4) are equally threatening and in common with other pictures of the period, have a peculiarly three-dimensional feel, giving the impression that the scene could be reconstructed from sprung steel. The foreground structures suggest military guns while the scalloped white shapes at the top of the picture hint at coastal cliffs, primed against attack. An unusual (perhaps unique) feature is the seven-sided hardboard frame, stuck on to the canvas to underscore the dynamism and modernity of the compo-sition. *Mediterranean Hill Town* of 1923 (plate 5) is undoubtedly one of McCance's most successful landscape paintings and was begun after visiting the small town of Bogliasco in Italy, its viaduct visible in the distance. The curved and cubic structures are fitted together with great mastery, making the hillside seem almost like a living, breathing organism, bursting with energy.

How did McCance make the leap from the representational pictures of his student days to these demonstrably modernist paint-ings? Clearly the answer lies in Cubism and the offshoots it produced in the years around 1910–20. McCance's work bears some for-mal resemblance to pre-war Cubist painting, for example that of Léger, Picabia, le Fau-connier and Gleizes, in the way in which objects are shorn of detail and treated as fac-eted, volumetric planes. His paintings may also be compared to those produced by the London based Vorticists, notably Wyndham Lewis, David Bomberg and William Roberts. McCance would certainly have known their work and may well have seen the Wyndham Lewis exhibition held at the Leicester Gal-leries in London in 1921. In 1924 William Roberts rented a room in McCance's Earl's Court flat[3] and at about the same time Mc-Cance and the sculptor Eric Kennington (who also favoured a style derived from Cubism) became good friends. *Boat Yard* (plate 6) has a marked resemblance to a lithograph by C. R. W. Nevinson, *Timber Loading at Southampton Docks* of 1917.[4] Yet although there are common threads with Vorticist and other Modernist tendencies in British art, McCance's work can stand entirely on its own terms. The *Boat Yard* picture is far more dynamic than Nevinson's print, having a highly animated sense of three dimensional form. It is this ability to convey the solidity and sculptural weight of forms, to give them a sense of urgent, thrusting movement, that really sets McCance's art apart.

His figure paintings are more clearly related to Wyndham Lewis's and there are also similarities with Leon Underwood's work. In the early 1920s McCance began to schematize the human body, stripping it of detail until it acquired an almost robotic appearance. The intense green and red skin tones served to accentuate this. *The Awakening* (plate 7) is one of several oils, including *Group from a Dream* and *Approaching Storm*, which feature vividly coloured nudes in landscape settings. Specific narratives seem to be suggested, though precisely what these might be remains a mystery. The figures in the background appear to be making gestures but are half obscured by the two nudes in front, caught in curiously contorted postures. These poses have clearly been chosen to provide a compositional structure and give an idea of movement being made in opposing directions, but the resulting picture adds up to far more than this. It is the awkward rigidity, the ambiguity, the strangeness which makes the painting so intriguing.

In the self portrait *The Result* (plate 8) (the title refers to the results page of the newspaper) the vertical sculpture seen in *Conflict* reappears on a table in the background. The angles of the walls and the perspective in the room have been distorted in an unsettling way while the colours are violently bright. The *Portrait of Joseph Brewer* (cover illustration) is perhaps the most assured of these man-machine portraits, many of which depict figures reading (no doubt reflecting McCance's own interest in writing and book design). Brewer was an American who was secretary to the editor of *The Spectator* in the mid-twenties during which time, from May 1923 to July 1926, McCance acted as the magazine's art critic.

In his reviews McCance discussed the work of Picasso, Kennington, Dobson and Rodin among others, but generally his observations were of a discursive nature, broaching wide ranging issues in the visual arts. He voiced opinions on sculpture, the design of motor cars, furniture, pottery (he was an early admirer of Bernard Leach and Shoji Hamada), advertising posters, painting and the cinema, and did so incisively, drawing upon an impressive background knowledge of each art. Refreshingly realistic in his attitude, he argued in favour of an interaction between art and industry, chastising those artists who thought themselves above working in advertising and poster design: 'For too long the artist has been regarded as a little "tin-god"; to be accepted as an honest tradesman and for art to be again placed on the footing of sound craftsmanship as it was in the Middle Ages is perhaps one of the healthiest signs of our time.'[5]

His art criticism seems to have brought him more recognition at the time than did his painting, and indeed at no point in his articles did he hint that he might be a practising artist. Through his writing, contacts with a number of artists and writers, such as Stanley Spencer, Eric Kennington, T. E. Lawrence, Edward McKnight Kauffer and Walter Pach were established. McCance also became acquainted with leading contemporary Scottish figures, including A. S. Neill

(the founding father of liberal child education), Naomi Mitchison, Edwin Muir and the
composer Francis George Scott whom he
had first met in 1916 at the Kennedy Street
School in Glasgow where Scott taught.

Like Muir and Francis George Scott,
McCance became involved in the 'Scottish
Renaissance' movement then being orches-
trated by the poet, essayist and man of letters
C. M. Grieve, better known under the *nom
de plume* of Hugh MacDiarmid. MacDiarmid's aim was to encourage and nurture a

specifically Scottish culture, independent of
the dominant English trends, and to this end
he wrote extensively in Lowland Scots dia-
lect. The first to draw critical attention to
McCance's work, he announced in a 1925
article on Edwin Muir that McCance was
'a profound critic and creative theorist, and a
brilliant artist of the latest school.'[6] Later that
year, MacDiarmid wrote a piece devoted
exclusively to McCance and Miller Parker,
hailing them as 'the most promising pheno-
mena of contemporary Scotland in regard to

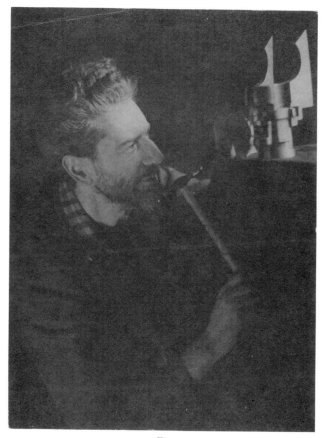

Fig 4
WILLIAM MCCANCE
c. 1925. *The sculpture was intended as a car mascot*

art . . . the lines along which they are now thinking and acting adumbrate the future of Scottish art.'[7]

In August 1925, MacDiarmid wrote to the publishers Blackwood and Son in the hope of starting up a publication on contemporary Scottish art and proposed that McCance, 'an ultra-modern artist of exceptional quality', should be art critic of the magazine which he himself would edit.[8] He also invited the artist to collaborate with him and Francis George Scott in creating some Scottish ballets.[9] McCance was ideally suited to MacDiarmid's plans for a 'Scottish Renaissance', being artistically gifted and intellectually adept – and of course, Scottish. Oddly though, at this stage it seems that MacDiarmid had not yet even met McCance, nor had he seen any of his work except in photographs.[10] Even so, MacDiarmid already considered McCance's work to be of central importance to the movement and he wrote to him, urging they keep in close contact: 'The whole idea of a Scottish Renaissance has reached a stage when . . . it needs those capable of forwarding it being in close personal touch with each other'.[11] He further requested McCance produce a frontispiece and illustrations for his forthcoming poem *A Drunk Man Looks at the Thistle*, now recognized as one of the great poetic works of the century, but the project did not bear fruit. The relationship was not simply one of MacDiarmid guiding and managing McCance. In 1928 McCance produced a painting *From Another Window in Thrums* (plate 9) (a witty lampoon on J. M. Barrie's sentimental novel *A Window in Thrums*) which preceded MacDiarmid's poem of the same name, first published in 1930.[12] A few years later, MacDiarmid wrote

to McCance requesting he send him some drawings so that he might write poems to them.[13]

Through MacDiarmid, McCance met James Whyte, editor of the magazine *The Modern Scot* (subtitled 'The Organ of the Scottish Renaissance'), for which McCance provided an article entitled 'Idea in Art', published in the summer 1930 issue. The text certainly owes something to MacDiarmid's thoughts and ends with a resounding plea for Scots to take art seriously and abandon provincialism: 'When the Scot can purge himself of the illusion that Art is reserved for the sentimentalist and realise that he, the Scot, has a natural gift for construction, combined with a racial aptitude for metaphysical thought and a deep emotional nature, then out of this combination can arise an art which will be pregnant with Idea, and have within it the seed of greatness.'[14]

Besides producing paintings of undoubted originality, McCance was also a prolific and inventive printmaker and it was in the direction of printing and typography that his career would ultimately lead. Wood engraving was experiencing a revival in Britain in the 1920s with artists such as Eric Ravilious, Iain Macnab, Robert Gibbings, Paul Nash and Blair Hughes Stanton excelling in this medium. Linocut also came into vogue, championed by Claude Flight, Sybil Andrews and the Grosvenor School artists.[15] Agnes Miller Parker was an immensely talented wood engraver whose finely hatched technique may have influenced McCance's own work in the early 1930s when their engravings became quite difficult to tell apart. In the 1920s however, McCance was more interested in Cubist effects and produced a series of linocuts which play on flattened, fragmented forms of machine-like character, for example *Tree Trunk Composition* of *c.* 1924 (fig 5).[16] The print is based on an oil painting of the same name which has a strong sense of spatial recession but in the linocut, McCance exploited the effects of contrast given by the medium to produce an almost abstract design.

McCance's drawings of the twenties can be fitted into two broad categories: charcoal or chalk figure and portrait drawings; and pencil still lifes and compositions. The charcoal drawings like *Study for a Colossal Steel Head* (fig 6) (possibly a study for a sculpture) have a very powerful three-dimensional quality and developed sense of form. The still lifes are more obviously Cubist in appearance, for example the 1927 pencil drawing *Early Telephone* (fig 7). Here, forms

are cut up, repeated and rearranged very much in the manner of Picasso and Braque's pre-war Cubist paintings.

McCance exhibited infrequently. He participated twice in shows in Glasgow in 1919 and 1920 and produced a large mural for the *Daily News* stand at the 1924 Wembley exhibition, but otherwise kept a low profile in terms of showing his own work.[17] He first exhibited at a London Gallery in 1928, when he and Miller Parker joined forces with another married couple, Blair Hughes Stanton and Gertrude Hermes, in a show at the St George's Gallery in central London.[18] Hughes Stanton and Hermes were wood engravers (Hermes was also a sculptor) producing finely-detailed prints quite similar to those of Agnes Miller Parker, and McCance had already written approvingly of their

Fig 5
TREE TRUNK COMPOSITION
c. 1924. Linocut on linen, 18.3 x 24.4 cm
(Private Collection)

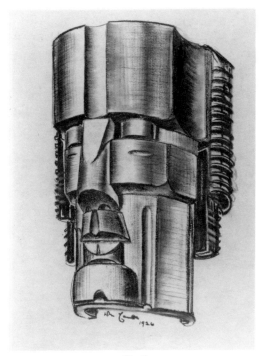

Fig 6
STUDY FOR A COLOSSAL STEEL HEAD
1926. Charcoal on paper, 53.6 x 37.6 cm
(Scottish National Gallery of Modern Art)

work in one of his *Spectator* articles. In 1930 McCance was one of ten artists exhibiting under the self-consciously modern title 'The Neo Society' at the Godfrey Phillips Gallery, with other artists including Miller Parker and Leon Underwood,[19] and in 1935 he participated in an exhibition of contemporary Scottish Art at James Whyte's Gallery in Saint Andrews.[20] Underwood had taught Hughes Stanton, Hermes and Henry Moore at the Brook Green School in the 1920s and together with Miller Parker, McCance, Lewis, Kennington, Roberts and others, it can be seen that there was a quite distinct artistic milieu operating in London at the time. A good many artists and writers lived in the Hammersmith area in west London, and McCance and Miller Parker lived in the same part of town, staying at Earl's Court from 1920–25 and then in Chiswick until 1929.

By 1930, Blair Hughes Stanton had acquired a growing reputation for his wood engravings and in that year was approached to succeed Robert Maynard as controller of the Gregynog Press in Newtown, Montgomeryshire (now Powys). When he chose instead to become the principal engraver, McCance was suggested as a suitable candidate[21] and after a trip to Gregynog to meet its Directors, was duly appointed controller of the Press. The foursome, McCance, Miller Parker, Hughes Stanton and Gertrude

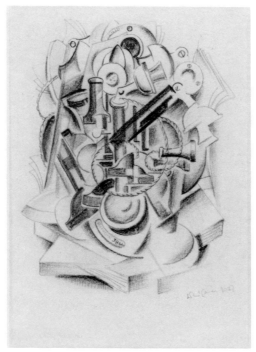

Fig 7
EARLY TELEPHONE
1927. Pencil on paper, 22 x 16 cm
(Private Collection)

Hermes, left London for Gregynog in October 1930, the two women also taking salaried positions as wood engravers.

The Gregynog Press had been founded by the sisters Gwendoline and Margaret Davies, grand-daughters of the wealthy industrialist David Davies. Together they formed an impressive art collection and funded artistic and social causes in Wales, promoting musical activities in particular.[22] They purchased the Gregynog estate in 1919 with the intention that it become a centre for the promotion of Welsh culture and in 1922 acquired a press for the printing of high quality books and pamphlets. The standard of craftsmanship, from handmade paper to fine illustrations

and bindings, was impeccable and was matched only by the Ashendene and Golden Cockerel Presses in England. At its peak in the early 1930s, seventeen craftsmen and women were employed by the Gregynog Press, producing books in editions normally of about 250 copies. For some of these editions, a small number were given sumptuous leather or sheepskin bindings with hand-tooled cover designs.

The choice of McCance to run the Press was a bold one since he had no previous experience in administrative work of this kind and no formal training in matters of typography. Nor indeed had Hughes Stanton, so they were both dispatched elsewhere for a

Fig 8
HERTE AND DOGGES
1931. *By Agnes Miller Parker*
Wood engraving, 10.8 x 12.7 cm
(Scottish National Gallery of Modern Art)

Fig 9
INITIAL LETTER S
FROM THE FABLES OF ESOPE
1932. Wood engraving, 4.7 x 4.7 cm
(Private Collection)

month to learn the basic techniques. The choice was an inspired one however, for the books produced under McCance's controllership are among the finest made by any of the Private Presses operating in Britain. The first book to be produced under his direction was Milton's *Comus* printed in 1931 in an edition of 250 with illustrations by Hughes Stanton. Caxton's translation of *The Fables of Esope* followed in 1932[23] with superb wood engravings by Miller Parker (fig 8), accompanied by McCance's delightful initial letters (fig 9). He also designed the cover for the de-luxe version of the edition.

The position of controller involved Mc-Cance in much tedious administrative work and he had little opportunity to execute illustrations, a task which fell mainly to Hughes Stanton. McCance did make sketches, designs and an ambitious lay-out for the Old Testament book of *Job* but unfortunately it was never printed. In 1932 he produced initial letters, frontispiece and a stunning cover design for Sir Robert Vansittart's *The Singing Caravan*, a project which involved much correspondence between the two men and which developed into a warm friendship. O. M. Edwards' *Clych Atgof* (Bells of Memory) was printed in Welsh in 1933 and featured a frontispiece by McCance. In all, a total of nine books was produced during his period as controller from 1930 to 1933 in addition to scores of pamphlets, Orders of Service and assorted ephemera. Arguably this was the high-point in the history of the Press which produced its last book in 1940 and did not survive the war.

Living on the Gregynog estate was a claustrophobic experience and the years spent there were difficult ones for all concerned. Hughes Stanton left Gertrude Hermes for another woman, causing a good deal of ill feeling on all sides. Rifts also emerged between McCance and the Board of Directors. Hughes Stanton's extra-marital activities resulted in the termination of his contract, at which point McCance and Miller Parker also decided to move on.

In October 1933 they left Gregynog for a converted windmill at Albrighton, near Wolverhampton, where they lived for three years. Agnes Miller Parker taught part-time at Newport Grammar School and McCance also did occasional work there. Never one to adhere to convention, his chief interest now shifted from typography to economic theory. In Wales he had given lectures on matters of contemporary economics and on moving he joined and became vice-chair-

Fig 10
SCOTS!UNITE!
1933. Published in *The Free Man*

man of the Wolverhampton branch of the Douglas Social Credit Group. The group's theories were based on ideas expounded by Major C. H. Douglas, a Scottish engineer, and their principal goal was to achieve a radical change in the credit policy of banks. During the economically unstable years between the wars, the Douglas movement became a potent and powerful force, attracting committed support from Ezra Pound, Hugh MacDiarmid, Edwin Muir and many Socialist intellectuals. The review *The New Age* became the mouthpiece of the move-

Fig 11
RECLINING FIGURE
1935. Fireclay, 19 x 26.5 x 20 cm
(Private Collection)

ment, as did the Scottish magazines *The Modern Scot* and *The Free Man* (the latter was edited by MacDiarmid). McCance delivered lectures on the subject and wrote a lengthy manifesto-like essay in which he attacked the harmful effects of credit policy on contemporary society. At MacDiarmid's invitation he produced two cartoons on the theme of banking, both of which were published in *The Free Man*. The first one delighted Mac-Diarmid who wrote to McCance asking for more: 'Can you help . . . with something that hits the nails both of Nationalism and Finance . . . Let me know if you can manage us summat.'[24] McCance obliged with the cartoon *Scots! Unite!* (fig 10) published in the issue of 4 February 1933 in which a Scot is shown chained to the Kafkaesque machinery of the banking system. Following Douglas's

observations, all the profits are syphoned off as 'Surplus' while 'Purchasing Power' is represented by a tiny collecting box.

Due to the heavy workload at Gregynog, McCance had stopped painting altogether, channelling his efforts instead into his wood engravings and typographic layouts. He had, however, found time to produce a few intriguing figurative sculptures and he continued this interest at Albrighton, profiting from the proximity of a brickworks where he could make and fire clay sculptures (fig 11). These heavy-limbed figures of the mid 1930s were executed in a gritty fireclay and share certain features with contemporary sculptures by Henry Moore and Frank Dobson.

McCance and Miller Parker left the windmill in 1936 and moved to a rented bungalow at Hambleden, near Henley on Thames, not far from Eric Kennington's home at Ipsden in Oxfordshire. Shortly after the move, McCance recommended his art criticism, writing for various publications including *News Chronicle* and *Picture Post*. His articles on Jacob Epstein published in 1937 and 1939 provoked an appreciative letter from the sculptor, who reprinted them in his autobiography.[25] Since the early 1920s McCance had been planning a major treatise on art, a synopsis of which was printed in MacDiarmid's 1925 article. The 85,000 word typescript, eventually completed in 1941, offered a stimulating survey of the history of art through to Surrealism and also broached general matters such as the role of colour, artistic creativity and the interface between art and design. Unfortunately it failed to attract a publisher.

In 1944 McCance was appointed Lecturer in Typography and Book Production at the School of Art at Reading University, a position previously held by the printmaker Robert Gibbings. A year later, immediately war was over, he and a colleague travelled to France where they saw the celebrated cave paintings at Lascaux. The experience conspired with another event of that year, the apocalyptic bombing of Hiroshima, to provide inspiration for a new series of paintings – his first since the 1920s. In *Hiroshima* (also known as *Atom Horizon*) (plate 10) of 1947, one of his own fireclay sculptures reclines in the foreground next to an egg while in the distance, a darkened sun hangs heavily over a devastated landscape. A neolithic Venus figure appears in the opposite corner, symbol of the birth of civilization – now facing its greatest threat. *Still Life: The Fall*

(plate 11), also of 1947, features an egg and a half-eaten apple lying between massive fireclay figures representing Adam and Eve. Beyond, seen through a picture mount, are two standing figures, and to the right, a wizened tree, emblematic of a post-nuclear Eden. Although markedly different from the 1920s paintings it is interesting that McCance had returned to the practice, adopted in works such as *Conflict*, of basing the composition around his own sculptures. A substantial body of wax-resist watercolours and linocuts also evolved from the same sources, based again on the fireclay sculptures seen in landscape settings.

The relationship between McCance and Agnes Miller Parker had not been without tension and in 1955 they separated, she returning to Scotland and eventually settling on the Isle of Arran while he moved into Reading. His first solo exhibition was held at Reading Museum and Art Gallery in 1960 and featured over two hundred items. He retired that same year and in 1963, following his marriage to Dr Margaret Chislett, a colleague at Reading University, moved back to Scotland, settling at Girvan in Ayrshire. In his last years he reprinted many of the linocuts of the 1920s using an old wooden mangle and also produced a new series of abstract watercolours using the wax-resist technique. He also made a few oil paintings, including *Diks Rac* ('Car Skid' backwards) (plate 12) of 1961 which shows the mangled remains of a crashed car reduced to a near abstract schema. Following a persistent lung infection, William McCance died in 1970 at the age of 76, his position as one of the foremost modern Scottish artists having been largely forgotten.

NOTES

1. The precise date of their move to London is not known. McCance was discharged at the end of March 1920, but in the 1930 *Neo Society* exhibition catalogue describes himself as having left Scotland 'on holiday' in 1919. He was certainly in London by 1920 when he produced illustrations for *Lloyd's Magazine* under the name of 'Mack'.

2. A date of 1920 for *Conflict* was put forward in the catalogues of the McCance exhibitions at Reading (1960) and Dundee (1975).

3. A certain amount of friction was caused when Roberts's rental cheque of December 1924 bounced.

4. The similarity was pointed out to me by William Hardie.

5. 'Art & Commerce' in *The Spectator*, 4 April 1925.

6. *The Scottish Educational Journal*, 4 Sept 1925. Reprinted in C. M. Grieve, *Contemporary Scottish Studies* (London 1926), p.111.

7. *The Scottish Educational Journal*, 20 Nov 1925. Reprinted in *Contemporary Scottish Studies*, (op.cit.), pp.184-190.

8. Letter of 14 August 1925 reprinted in Alan Bold (ed.), *The Letters of Hugh MacDiarmid* (London 1984), pp.338-41.

9. Letter to Mr Ogilvie, probably November 1925, reprinted in Alan Bold (op.cit.), pp.85-6. A report on the proposal was carried in *The Daily Chronicle*, 2 December 1925. The project did not, however, materialize.

10. See letter of 22 Nov 1925 (This and all subsequent MacDiarmid/McCance correspondence mentioned here are presently deposited at the National Library of Scotland (Acc. no. 9891)). MacDiarmid asked McCance to correct any errors in the article before it was reprinted in *Contemporary Scottish Studies* and requested some photos of his work. He declared: 'It is difficult writing about people and people's work one doesn't know'. In his 1925 writings on McCance, MacDiarmid incorrectly referred to him as 'Professor McCance'.

11. Letter from MacDiarmid to McCance, 12 March 1926.

12. MacDiarmid's 'Frae Anither Window in Thrums' was published in 1930 in the collection entitled *To Circumjack Cencrastus*, but it may have been written some time earlier. An article by MacDiarmid on McCance's painting was published in *The Glasgow Evening News* (Saturday supplement), 7 June 1930.

13. Letter from MacDiarmid to McCance, 1 Oct 1931.

14. *The Modern Scot*, Vol II, Summer 1930, pp.13-16

15. See the catalogue *The Grosvenor School: British Linocuts between the Wars*, Rhode Island School of Design Museum, 1988.

16. McCance's prints are impossible to date with any certainty. Although some are signed and dated, many copies were actually printed in the 1960s and the datings then given may be incorrect.

17. He showed works at the Glasgow Society of Painters and Sculptors exhibitions of 1919 and 1920 at the McLellan Galleries, Glasgow. The Wembley frieze measured 50 foot in length and was titled 'First with the News'.

18. St George's Gallery, 32a George Street, London w1, Feb-March 1928. The four exhibited a total of 85 works. McCance showed paintings, drawings and sculptures.

19. 9 May–7 June 1930, at 43 Duke Street, London sw1. This was the first and only show of the group. McCance showed a total of ten works.

20. Other artists exhibiting included Percy Bliss, James Cowie, William Johnstone, Hugh Adam Crawford and Maclauchlan Milne.

21. McCance credited the connoisseur and collector Hugh Blaker for putting his name forward. Dorothy A. Harrop in *A History of Gregynog Press* (Private Libraries Association, 1980) reports that Hughes Stanton suggested McCance for the appointment.

22. The sisters left their important collection of Impressionist paintings to the National Museum of Wales.

23. Although the edition is dated 1931 it was actually printed in 1932.

24. Letter from MacDiarmid to McCance, 5 Jan 1933.

25. 'Leave Epstein Alone' in *News Chronicle* 28 Nov 1937 and 'Epstein's Adam' in *Picture Post* 24 June 1939. Both reprinted in Jacob Epstein, *Let There be Sculpture*, London 1942.

PLATES

1. Seascape, *c.* 1920-23
Oil on wood, 24 x 30.5 cm
(Private Collection)

2. Primeval Movement, *c.* 1922
Oil on card, 23 x 25 cm
(Private Collection)

3. Conflict, 1922

Oil on canvas, 100.5 x 87.5 cm

(Glasgow Art Gallery and Museums)

4. Heavy Structures in a Landscape Setting, 1922
Oil on canvas, maximum visible surface, 68 x 82 cm
(Private Collection)

5. Mediterranean Hill Town, 1923
Oil on canvas, 92.1 x 61 cm
(Dundee Art Galleries and Museums)

6. Boat Yard, *c.* 1922
Oil on canvas, 64 x 77 cm
(Mr and Mrs William Hardie)

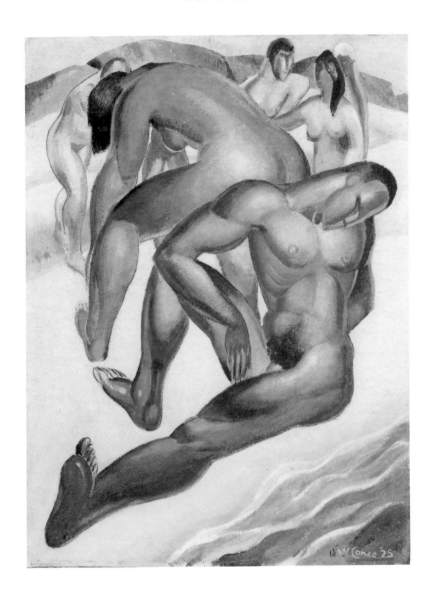

7. The Awakening, 1925
Oil on board, 61 x 46 cm
(Private Collection)

8. The Result, *c.* 1924
Oil on canvas , 72 x 92 cm
(Robert Fleming Holdings Limited)

9. From Another Window in Thrums, 1928
Oil on board, 60 x 46 cm
(Graeme Mundy Gallery Ltd, Glasgow)

10. Hiroshima (Atom Horizon), 1947
Oil on board, 46 x 61 cm
(Private Collection)

11. Still Life: The Fall, 1947
Oil on canvas, 72 x 59 cm
(Private Collection)

12. Diks Rac, 1961

Oil on board, 61 x 45 cm

(Private Collection)

SELECT BIBLIOGRAPHY

C. M. Grieve (Hugh MacDiarmid), 'William and Agnes M'Cance' in *Scottish Educational Journal*, 20 Nov 1925, reprinted in C. M. Grieve, *Contemporary Scottish Studies* (Leonard Parsons, London, 1926), pp.184-190

St George's Gallery, London, *Blair Hughes Stanton, William M'Cance, Gertrude Hermes, Agnes Millar-Parker*. Exhibition catalogue, Feb–March 1928

Godfrey Phillips Galleries, London, *The Neo Society*. Exhibition catalogue, 9 May–7 June 1930

Hugh MacDiarmid, 'The Art of William McCance' in *Saltire Review*, 22, 1960, pp.24-27

Reading Museum and Art Gallery, *Works by William McCance*. Exhibition catalogue 1960

Girvan Town Council, *William McCance*. Exhibition catalogue, 1972 (introduction by Hugh MacDiarmid)Dundee Museums and Art Gallery, *William McCance (1894-1970)*. Exhibition catalogue, 1975

William Hardie, *Scottish Painting 1837-1939*, London, 1976. (revised as *Scottish Art from 1837 to the Present*, 1990)

Scottish Arts Council, *Graven Images: The Art of British Wood Engraving*. Exhibition catalogue, 1979

Dorothy A. Harrap, *A History of Gregynog Press* (Private Libraries Association, 1980)

Alan Bold (ed.), *The Letters of Hugh MacDiarmid* (London 1984)

Scottish National Gallery of Modern Art, *Scottish Art Since 1900*. Exhibition catalogue, 1989

PUBLISHED WRITINGS BY WILLIAM McCANCE

The Spectator. Articles in the following issues:
1923: 26 May, 24 Nov, 15 Dec.
1924: 26 April, 10 May, 17 May, 14 June, 12 July, 18 Oct, 22 Nov, 20 Dec.
1925: 10 Jan, 31 Jan, 14 Feb, 21 Feb, 4 April, 25 April, 9 May, 13 June, 18 July, 17 Oct, 21 Nov, 12 Dec.
1926: 16 Jan, 23 Jan, 27 Feb, 13 March, 24 April, 15 May, 5 June, 19 June, 24 July

The Modern Scot, Summer 1930 (vol.II), 'Idea in Art'

The Queen, 6 May 1937, 'A critic compares kings in sculpture'

News Chronicle, 28 Oct 1937, 'Leave Epstein Alone'

News Chronicle, 10 March 1938, 'If we don't use our hands'

Reynolds News, 7 Aug 1938 'When, why and how Scotland laughs'

Reynolds News, 8 Jan 1939, 'Battle of Ideas: Democracy and the ordinary man'

Reynolds News, 15 Jan 1939, 'My Scotland: Our art tradition'

Picture Post, 24 June 1939, 'Epstein's Adam'

Picture Post, 6 Jan 1940, 'Lawrence R.I.P.'

Picture Post, 20 April 1940, 'Just a Farm Labourer'

Picture Post, 20 July 1940, 'Surrealism'

Picture Post, 10 August 1940, 'Mrs Cook, the village artist'

Reynolds News, 13 April 1941, 'Spring Symphony of the Country'

Britansky Soyusnik (British Ally), 2 Oct 1946, 'Typography'

Universities Quarterly, Feb 1953, 'Printing in the services of universities'

Architectural Design, March 1960, 'The influence of Cubism on Garden Design' (with H. F. Clark)

Delta, Autumn 1963, 'The Grate: a Short Story'